Contents

You're Why I Bake a Duncan Hines Dessert.

What could be sweeter than giving and sharing a home-baked dessert with loved ones? Whether it's the quality time you spend baking together, the pleasure on their faces when you present them with an unexpected homemade treat, or simply the fun you have enjoying the results, Duncan Hines can be a delicious part of family togetherness. And to keep things interesting, Duncan Hines has created this cookbook, Baking With Love, to offer new ways to say, "You're Why I Bake."

For generations, moms have relied on the premium quality and convenience of Duncan Hines to create superior results without the extra effort. While improving upon the time tested quality of Duncan Hines desserts was a challenge, our kitchen staff was able to develop more than 70 recipes that bring mouthwatering new twists to old favorites. Simply adding almond flavor to our Duncan Hines Angel Food Cake mix, for example, results in heavenly Angel Almond Cupcakes.

Mixing candied cherries and chocolate chips with our Golden Sugar Cookie mix turns a classic cookie into a Cherry Surprise worthy of the name.

Whether baking for the first time or the hundredth, our easy-to-follow instructions ensure that it takes little time and effort to serve a deeply satisfying dessert. After mastering these recipes, even less experienced bakers might be inspired to create their own customized Duncan Hines treats.

Remember, you don't need a special reason to bake, you just need a special person. And doesn't that special person deserve the moistness and irresistible taste of Duncan Hines cakes, cookies, and brownies? After all, life is better when it's full of sweet surprises.

Luscious
LAYER CAKES

Autumn Gold Pumpkin Cake

1 package DUNCAN
   HINES Moist Deluxe
   Butter Recipe
   Golden Cake Mix
3 eggs
1 cup water
1 cup solid pack pumpkin
1½ teaspoons ground
   cinnamon, divided

¼ teaspoon *each:* ground
   ginger and nutmeg
1 cup chopped walnuts
1 container DUNCAN
   HINES Vanilla
   Frosting
¼ cup coarsely chopped
   walnuts for garnish

Preheat oven to 375°F. Grease and flour two 8-inch round cake pans. Combine cake mix, eggs, water, pumpkin, 1 teaspoon cinnamon, ginger and nutmeg in large mixing bowl. Beat at medium speed with electric mixer for 4 minutes. Stir in 1 cup walnuts. Pour into prepared pans. Bake 30 to 35 minutes or until toothpick inserted in center comes out clean. Cool in pans 15 minutes. Remove from pans. Cool completely. Combine frosting and remaining ½ teaspoon cinnamon. Stir until blended. Fill and frost cake. Garnish with ¼ cup walnuts.   *Makes 12 to 16 servings*

Chocolate Toffee Cream Cake

1 package DUNCAN HINES
    Moist Deluxe Dark
    Chocolate Fudge Cake
    Mix
3 eggs
1⅓ cups water
½ cup vegetable oil

1 (6-ounce) package milk
    chocolate English toffee
    chips, divided
1 (12-ounce) container extra
    creamy non-dairy
    whipped topping,
    thawed

Preheat oven to 350°F. Grease and flour two 9-inch round cake pans.

Blend cake mix, eggs, water and oil in large mixing bowl until moistened. Beat at medium speed with electric mixer for 4 minutes. Pour into prepared pans. Bake 30 to 33 minutes or until toothpick inserted in center comes out clean. Cool in pans 15 minutes. Remove from pans. Cool completely. Reserve ¼ cup toffee chips; fold remaining chips into whipped topping. Place one cake layer on serving plate; spread with ¾ cup topping mixture. Top with remaining layer. Frost sides and top with remaining topping mixture; garnish with reserved chips. Refrigerate until ready to serve.

Makes 12 to 16 servings

TIP

If chocolate toffee chips are not available, 4 chocolate covered toffee candy bars can be substituted. Chop bars in a food processor until small pieces form.

Chocolate Toffee Cream Cake

Strawberry Raspberry Cake

1 package DUNCAN HINES
Moist Deluxe Strawberry
Supreme Cake Mix
2 ounces white chocolate
baking bar, grated,
divided

½ cup red raspberry jam
1 container DUNCAN
HINES Vanilla Frosting
Red raspberries (optional)

Preheat oven to 350°F. Grease and flour two 9-inch round cake pans.

Prepare cake mix as directed on package. Stir in ½ cup grated chocolate. Set aside remaining chocolate for garnish. Bake 28 to 31 minutes or until toothpick inserted in center comes out clean. Cool in pans 15 minutes. Invert onto cooling racks. Cool completely. Place one cake layer on serving plate. Spread with jam. Top with second cake layer. Frost sides and top of cake with frosting. Garnish with remaining grated chocolate and raspberries.

Makes 12 to 16 servings

Chocolate Dream Torte

1 package DUNCAN HINES
Moist Deluxe Dark
Chocolate Fudge Cake
Mix
1 (6-ounce) package
semisweet chocolate
chips, melted
1 (8-ounce) container frozen
non-dairy whipped
topping, thawed, divided

1 container DUNCAN
HINES Milk Chocolate
Frosting
3 tablespoons finely chopped
dry roasted pistachios

Preheat oven to 350°F. Grease and flour two 9-inch round cake pans.

Prepare, bake and cool cake as directed on package for basic recipe.

For chocolate hearts garnish, spread melted chocolate to ⅛-inch thickness on waxed paper-lined baking sheet. Cut shapes with heart cookie cutter when chocolate begins to set. Refrigerate until firm. Push out heart shapes. Set aside.

To assemble, split each cake layer in half horizontally. Place one split cake layer on serving plate. Spread one-third of whipped topping on top. Repeat with remaining layers and whipped topping, leaving top plain. Frost sides and top with frosting. Sprinkle pistachios on top. Position chocolate hearts by pushing points down into cake. Refrigerate until ready to serve.   *Makes 12 to 16 servings*

Mocha Fudge Cake

1 package DUNCAN HINES Moist Deluxe Butter Recipe Fudge Cake Mix	1 tablespoon instant coffee granules
1 cup hot fudge ice cream topping	4 cups frozen non-dairy whipped topping, thawed, divided

Preheat oven to 375°F. Grease and flour two 9-inch round cake pans.

Prepare, bake and cool cake as directed on package.

Combine hot fudge topping and coffee in medium saucepan. Heat until coffee crystals are dissolved. Cool. Fold 2 cups whipped topping into fudge topping mixture. Refrigerate 30 minutes.

Place one cake layer on serving plate. Spread with 1 cup filling. Top with second cake layer. Add remaining 2 cups whipped topping to remaining filling. Frost top and sides of cake with topping mixture.
           Makes 12 to 16 servings

Black Forest Torte

1 package DUNCAN HINES
   Moist Deluxe Dark
   Chocolate Fudge Cake
   Mix
2½ cups whipping cream,
   chilled

2½ tablespoons confectioners'
   sugar
1 (21-ounce) can cherry pie
   filling

Preheat oven to 350°F. Grease and flour two 9-inch round cake pans.

Prepare, bake and cool cake as directed on package.

Beat whipping cream in large bowl until soft peaks form. Add sugar gradually. Beat until stiff peaks form.

To assemble, place one cake layer on serving plate. Spread two-thirds cherry pie filling on cake to within ½ inch of edge. Spread 1½ cups whipped cream mixture over cherry pie filling. Top with second cake layer. Frost sides and top with remaining whipped cream mixture. Spread remaining cherry pie filling on top to within 1 inch of edge. Refrigerate until ready to serve.   *Makes 12 to 16 servings*

TIP

**Chill the cherry pie filling for easy
spreading on cake. Also, garnish the
cake with grated semisweet chocolate
or white chocolate curls.**

Black Forest Torte

Delicate White Chocolate Cake

1 package DUNCAN HINES Moist Deluxe Yellow Cake Mix
1 (4-serving size) package vanilla-flavor instant pudding and pie filling mix
4 egg whites
1 cup water
½ cup vegetable oil
5 ounces finely chopped white chocolate

1 cup cherry preserves
8 drops red food coloring (optional)
2 cups whipping cream, chilled
2 tablespoons confectioners' sugar
Maraschino cherries for garnish
1 ounce white chocolate shavings for garnish

Preheat oven to 350°F. Cut waxed paper circles to fit bottoms of three 9-inch round cake pans. Grease bottoms and sides of pans. Line with waxed paper circles.

Combine cake mix, pudding mix, egg whites, water and oil in large mixing bowl. Beat at medium speed with electric mixer for 2 minutes. Fold in chopped white chocolate. Pour into prepared pans. Bake 18 to 22 minutes or until toothpick inserted in center comes out clean. Cool in pans 15 minutes. Invert onto cooling racks. Peel off waxed paper. Cool completely.

Combine cherry preserves and food coloring, if desired. Stir to blend color.

Beat whipping cream in large bowl until soft peaks form. Add sugar gradually. Beat until stiff peaks form.

To assemble, place one cake layer on serving plate. Spread ½ cup cherry preserves over cake. Place second cake layer on top. Spread with remaining preserves. Place third cake layer on top. Frost sides and top of cake with whipped cream. Decorate with maraschino cherries and white chocolate shavings. Refrigerate until ready to serve.

Makes 12 to 16 servings

Delicate White Chocolate Cake

Chocolate Cherry Cake

1 package DUNCAN HINES Moist Deluxe Devil's Food Cake Mix ½ cup chopped maraschino cherries, well drained 2 cups frozen non-dairy whipped topping, thawed	1 container DUNCAN HINES Chocolate Frosting

Preheat oven to 350°F. Grease and flour two 9-inch round cake pans.

Prepare, bake and cool cake as directed on package. Fold maraschino cherries into whipped topping.

To assemble, place one cake layer on serving plate. Spread with whipped topping mixture. Top with second layer. Frost sides and top with frosting. Refrigerate until ready to serve.

Makes 12 to 16 servings

Tip: Fresh or canned dark sweet cherries, well drained, can be used in place of maraschino cherries.

Chocolate Peanut Butter Frosted Cake

1 package DUNCAN HINES Moist Deluxe Devil's Food Cake Mix 1⅓ cups water ½ cup vegetable oil 3 eggs	1 container DUNCAN HINES Chocolate Frosting ½ cup creamy peanut butter ½ cup chopped peanuts

Preheat oven to 350°F. Grease and lightly flour two 9-inch round cake pans.

Combine cake mix, water, oil and eggs in large mixing bowl. Beat at low speed with electric mixer until moistened. Beat at medium speed for 2 minutes. Pour into prepared pans. Bake 30 to 33 minutes or until toothpick inserted in center comes out clean. Cool in pans 15 minutes; remove from pans. Cool completely. Mix frosting and peanut butter in small bowl until smooth. Fill and frost cake. Sprinkle with peanuts. *Makes 12 to 16 servings*

Apricot Cream Cake

Cake

  1 package DUNCAN HINES
      Moist Deluxe Yellow
      Cake Mix

  1 (18-ounce) jar apricot
      preserves, divided

Frosting

  1 (4-serving size) package
      vanilla-flavor instant
      pudding and pie filling
      mix
  ¾ cup milk
  1½ cups whipping cream,
      chilled

  ¼ cup flaked coconut for
      garnish
  Apricot halves and mint
      leaves for garnish

Preheat oven to 350°F. Grease and flour two 9-inch round cake pans.

Prepare, bake and cool cake as directed on package. Split each cake layer in half horizontally. Reserve 1 tablespoon preserves. Place one split cake layer on serving plate. Spread one-third remaining preserves on top. Repeat with remaining layers and preserves, leaving top plain.

Prepare pudding mix as directed on package using ¾ cup milk. Beat whipping cream until stiff in large bowl. Fold whipped cream into pudding. Spread on sides and top of cake. Garnish with coconut, apricot halves and mint leaves. Warm reserved preserves to glaze apricot halves. Refrigerate until ready to serve. *Makes 12 servings*

Tip: Three cups thawed frozen non-dairy whipped topping may be substituted for whipping cream.

Cookies & Creme Cake

1 package DUNCAN HINES
   Moist Deluxe White
   Cake Mix
3 egg whites
1⅓ cups water
2 tablespoons vegetable oil
1 cup coarsely chopped
   creme-filled chocolate
   sandwich cookies (about
   12 cookies)

1 container DUNCAN
   HINES Butter Cream
   Frosting
Additional cookies
   (optional)

Preheat oven to 350°F. Grease and flour two 9-inch round cake pans.

Combine cake mix, egg whites, water and oil in large mixing bowl. Beat at low speed with electric mixer until moistened. Beat at medium speed for 2 minutes. Fold in 1 cup cookies. Pour into prepared pans. Bake 28 to 31 minutes or until toothpick inserted in center comes out clean. Cool in pans 15 minutes. Remove from pans; cool completely. Fill and frost cake with frosting. Garnish with additional cookies, if desired.

Makes 12 to 16 servings

TIP

To quickly chop cookies, place 6 cookies in food processor fitted with steel blade. Pulse several times until coarsely chopped. Repeat with remaining cookies.

Cookies & Creme Cake

Simply DELICIOUS CAKES

Chocolate Chip Cookie Cake

1 package DUNCAN HINES Moist Deluxe Yellow Cake Mix	½ cup water
	⅓ cup vegetable oil
1 (4-serving size) package vanilla-flavor instant pudding and pie filling mix	1 (12-ounce) package semisweet chocolate chips
	1½ cups finely chopped pecans
4 eggs	Confectioners' sugar for garnish

Preheat oven to 350°F. Grease and flour 10-inch Bundt pan.

Combine cake mix, pudding mix, eggs, water and oil in large mixing bowl. Beat at medium speed with electric mixer for 2 minutes. Stir in chips and pecans. Pour into prepared pan. Bake 50 to 60 minutes or until toothpick inserted in center comes out clean. Cool in pan 25 minutes. Invert onto serving plate. Cool completely. Dust with confectioners' sugar, if desired.   *Makes 12 to 16 servings*

Double Chocolate Snack Cake

1 package DUNCAN HINES
 Moist Deluxe Devil's
 Food Cake Mix
1 cup white chocolate chips,
 divided

½ cup semisweet chocolate
 chips

Preheat oven to 350°F. Grease and flour 13×9-inch pan.

Prepare cake mix as directed on package. Stir in ½ cup white chocolate chips and semisweet chips. Pour into prepared pan. Bake 35 to 40 minutes or until toothpick inserted in center comes out clean. Remove from oven; sprinkle top with remaining ½ cup white chocolate chips. Serve warm or cool completely in pan.

Makes 12 to 16 servings

TIP

**For a special dessert, serve cake warm
with a scoop of vanilla ice cream or
whipped cream garnished with
chocolate chips.**

Double Chocolate Snack Cake

Hot Fudge Pudding Cake

1 package DUNCAN HINES
  Moist Deluxe Devil's
  Food Cake Mix
2 eggs
1 cup water
1 cup chopped pecans
½ cup granulated sugar

½ cup packed brown sugar
2 tablespoons unsweetened
  cocoa powder
1 cup boiling water
  Whipped topping for
  garnish

Preheat oven to 350°F. Grease and flour 13×9-inch pan.

Combine cake mix, eggs and water in large mixing bowl. Beat at medium speed with electric mixer for 2 minutes. Stir in pecans. Pour into prepared pan.

Combine granulated sugar, brown sugar and cocoa in small bowl. Sprinkle over batter. Pour boiling water over all. *Do not stir.* Bake 45 minutes or until toothpick inserted in center halfway to bottom comes out clean. Serve warm with whipped topping.

Makes 12 to 16 servings

TIP

For a richer dessert, use DUNCAN HINES Moist Deluxe Dark Chocolate Cake Mix in place of Devil's Food Cake Mix.

Coconut Pound Cake

1 package DUNCAN HINES
  Moist Deluxe French
  Vanilla Cake Mix
1 (4-serving size) package
  coconut cream-flavor
  instant pudding and pie
  filling mix
4 eggs

1 cup water
⅓ cup vegetable oil
1 cup flaked coconut
1 cup confectioners' sugar
2 tablespoons milk
  Additional coconut for
  garnish

Preheat oven to 350°F. Grease and flour 10-inch Bundt pan.

Combine cake mix, pudding mix, eggs, water and oil in large mixing bowl. Beat at medium speed with electric mixer for 2 minutes. Fold in 1 cup coconut. Pour into prepared pan. Bake 45 to 50 minutes or until toothpick inserted in center comes out clean. Cool in pan 25 minutes. Invert onto serving plate. Mix sugar and milk in small bowl until smooth. Drizzle over cake. Sprinkle with additional coconut, if desired. *Makes 12 to 16 servings*

TIP

Garnish the top of the cake with toasted coconut. To toast coconut, spread on baking sheet and bake at 350°F for 3 minutes. Stir and bake 1 to 2 minutes longer or until light golden brown.

Upside-Down German Chocolate Cake

1½ cups flaked coconut
1½ cups chopped pecans
1 package DUNCAN HINES
    Moist Deluxe German
    Chocolate or Chocolate
    Cake Mix

1 (8-ounce) package cream
    cheese, softened
½ cup butter or margarine,
    melted
1 pound confectioners' sugar
    (3½ to 4 cups)

Preheat oven to 350°F. Grease and flour 13×9-inch pan.

Spread coconut evenly on bottom of pan. Sprinkle with pecans. Prepare cake mix as directed on package. Pour over coconut and pecans. Combine cream cheese and melted butter in medium mixing bowl. Beat at low speed with electric mixer until creamy. Add sugar; beat until blended and smooth. Drop by spoonfuls evenly over cake batter. Bake 45 to 50 minutes or until toothpick inserted halfway to bottom of cake comes out clean. Cool completely in pan. To serve, cut into individual pieces; turn upside down onto plate.

Makes 12 to 16 servings

TIP

**Cake can be served warm, if desired.
Also, store leftover coconut in the
refrigerator and use within four weeks.**

Upside-Down German Chocolate Cake

Blueberry Angel Food Cake Rolls

1 package DUNCAN HINES
Angel Food Cake Mix
¼ cup confectioners' sugar
plus additional for
dusting

1 (21-ounce) can blueberry
pie filling
Mint leaves for garnish

Preheat oven to 350°F. Line two 15½×10½×1-inch jelly-roll pans with aluminum foil.

Prepare cake mix as directed on package. Divide and spread evenly into pans. Cut through batter with knife or spatula to remove large air bubbles. Bake 15 minutes or until set. Invert cakes at once onto clean, lint-free dishtowels dusted with sugar. Remove foil carefully. Roll up each cake with towel jelly-roll fashion, starting at short end. Cool completely.

Unroll cakes. Spread about 1 cup blueberry pie filling to within 1 inch of edges on each cake. Reroll and place seam-side down on serving plate. Dust with ¼ cup sugar. Garnish with mint leaves, if desired.

Makes 2 cakes (8 servings each)

TIP

**For a variation in flavor, substitute
cherry pie filling for the blueberry
pie filling.**

Butter Pecan Banana Cake

Cake

1 package DUNCAN HINES
Moist Deluxe Butter
Recipe Golden Cake Mix
4 eggs
1 cup mashed ripe bananas
(about 3 medium)

¾ cup vegetable oil
½ cup granulated sugar
¼ cup milk
1 teaspoon vanilla extract
1 cup chopped pecans

Frosting

1 cup coarsely chopped
pecans
¼ cup butter or margarine

1 container DUNCAN
HINES Vanilla Frosting

Preheat oven to 325°F. Grease and flour 10-inch Bundt or tube pan.

Combine cake mix, eggs, bananas, oil, sugar, milk and vanilla extract in large mixing bowl. Beat at low speed with electric mixer until moistened. Beat at medium speed for 2 minutes. Stir in 1 cup chopped pecans. Pour into prepared pan. Bake 50 to 60 minutes or until toothpick inserted in center comes out clean. Cool in pan 25 minutes. Invert onto cooling rack. Cool completely.

Place 1 cup coarsely chopped pecans and butter in skillet. Cook on medium heat, stirring until pecans are toasted. Combine nut mixture and frosting in small bowl. Cool until spreading consistency. Frost cake.   *Makes 12 to 16 servings*

Lemon Crumb Cake

1 package DUNCAN HINES
   Moist Deluxe Lemon
   Supreme Cake Mix
3 eggs
1⅓ cups water
⅓ cup vegetable oil

1 cup all-purpose flour
½ cup packed light brown
   sugar
½ teaspoon baking powder
½ cup butter or margarine

Preheat oven to 350°F. Grease and flour 13×9-inch pan.

Combine cake mix, eggs, water and oil in large mixing bowl. Beat at medium speed with electric mixer for 2 minutes. Pour into prepared pan. Combine flour, sugar and baking powder in small bowl. Cut in butter until crumbly. Sprinkle evenly over batter. Bake 35 to 40 minutes or until toothpick inserted in center comes out clean. Cool completely in pan.

Makes 12 to 16 servings

TIP

Butter or margarine will cut easier into the flour mixture if it is chilled. Use two knives or a pastry cutter to cut the mixture into crumbs.

Lemon Crumb Cake

Strawberry Pound Cake

1 package DUNCAN HINES
  Moist Deluxe Strawberry
  Supreme Cake Mix
1 (4-serving size) package
  vanilla-flavor instant
  pudding and pie filling
  mix
4 eggs

1 cup water
⅓ cup vegetable oil
1 cup miniature semisweet
  chocolate chips
⅔ cup DUNCAN HINES
  Chocolate Butter Cream
  Frosting

Preheat oven to 350°F. Grease and flour 10-inch Bundt pan.

Combine cake mix, pudding mix, eggs, water and oil in large mixing bowl. Beat at low speed with electric mixer until moistened. Beat at medium speed for 2 minutes. Stir in chips. Pour into prepared pan. Bake 55 to 60 minutes or until toothpick inserted in center comes out clean. Cool in pan 25 minutes. Invert onto cooling rack. Cool completely.

Place frosting in 1-cup glass measuring cup. Microwave at HIGH for 10 to 15 seconds. Stir until smooth. Drizzle over top of cooled cake.

Makes 12 to 16 servings

TIP

Store leftover chocolate buttercream frosting, covered, in refrigerator. Spread frosting between graham crackers for a quick snack.

Strawberry Pound Cake

30

Carrot Cake

1 package DUNCAN HINES
   Moist Deluxe Yellow
   Cake Mix
2 cups grated fresh carrots
1 (8-ounce) can crushed
   pineapple with juice,
   undrained
½ cup water

3 eggs
½ cup vegetable oil
½ cup finely chopped pecans
2 teaspoons ground
   cinnamon
1 container DUNCAN
   HINES Cream Cheese
   Frosting

Preheat oven to 350°F. Grease and flour 13×9-inch pan.

Combine cake mix, carrots, pineapple with juice, water, eggs, oil, pecans and cinnamon in large mixing bowl. Beat at low speed with electric mixer until moistened. Beat at medium speed for 2 minutes. Pour into prepared pan. Bake 35 to 40 minutes or until toothpick inserted in center comes out clean. Cool in pan.

Spread frosting on cooled cake. Refrigerate until ready to serve.

Makes 12 to 16 servings

Chocolate Sock-It-to-Me Cake

1 package DUNCAN HINES Moist Deluxe Butter Recipe Fudge Cake Mix, divided	4 eggs
	1 cup sour cream
	⅓ cup vegetable oil
	¼ cup water
1 cup finely chopped pecans	¼ cup granulated sugar
2 tablespoons packed brown sugar	1 cup confectioners' sugar
	1 to 2 tablespoons milk

Preheat oven to 375°F. Grease and flour 10-inch tube pan.

Combine 2 tablespoons cake mix, pecans and brown sugar in medium bowl for streusel filling. Set aside.

Combine remaining cake mix, eggs, sour cream, oil, water and granulated sugar in large bowl. Beat at low speed with electric mixer until moistened. Beat at medium speed for 2 minutes. Pour two-thirds of batter into prepared pan. Sprinkle with streusel filling. Spoon remaining batter evenly over filling. Bake 45 to 55 minutes or until toothpick inserted in center comes out clean. Cool in pan 25 minutes. Invert onto cooling rack. Cool completely.

Combine confectioners' sugar and milk in small bowl. Stir until smooth. Drizzle over cake.   *Makes 12 to 16 servings*

TIP

For a quick glaze, heat ½ cup DUNCAN HINES Creamy Vanilla Frosting in a small saucepan over medium heat, stirring constantly, until thin. Drizzle over the cake.

Take-Along Cake

1 package DUNCAN HINES
    Moist Deluxe Swiss
    Chocolate Cake Mix
1 (12-ounce) package
    semisweet chocolate
    chips
1 cup miniature
    marshmallows

¼ cup butter or margarine,
    melted
½ cup packed brown sugar
½ cup chopped pecans or
    walnuts

Preheat oven to 350°F. Grease and flour 13×9-inch pan.

Prepare cake mix as directed on package. Add chips and
marshmallows to batter. Pour into prepared pan. Drizzle melted butter
over batter. Sprinkle with sugar and top with pecans. Bake 45 to 55
minutes or until toothpick inserted in center comes out clean. Serve
warm or cool completely in pan. *Makes 12 to 16 servings*

TIP

**To keep leftover pecans fresh,
store them in the freezer in an
airtight container.**

Take-Along Cake

Della Robbia Cake

1 package DUNCAN HINES
  Angel Food Cake Mix
1½ teaspoons grated lemon
  peel
1 cup water
6 tablespoons granulated
  sugar
1½ tablespoons cornstarch

1 tablespoon lemon juice
½ teaspoon vanilla extract
  Few drops red food
  coloring
6 cling peach slices
6 medium strawberries,
  sliced

Preheat oven to 375°F.

Prepare cake mix as directed on package, adding lemon peel. Bake and cool cake as directed on package.

Combine water, sugar and cornstarch in small saucepan. Cook on medium-high heat until mixture thickens and clears. Remove from heat. Stir in lemon juice, vanilla extract and food coloring.

Alternate peach slices with strawberry slices around top of cake. Pour glaze over fruit and top of cake.   *Makes 12 to 16 servings*

TIP

**For angel food cakes, always use a
totally grease-free cake pan to get the
best volume.**

Della Robbia Cake

Pineapple Orange Pound Cake

1 package DUNCAN HINES
   Moist Deluxe Pineapple
   Supreme Cake Mix
1 (4-serving size) package
   vanilla-flavor instant
   pudding and pie filling
   mix

4 eggs
1 cup plus 4 tablespoons
   orange juice, divided
⅓ cup vegetable oil
1 tablespoon grated orange
   peel
⅓ cup granulated sugar

Preheat oven to 350°F. Grease and flour 10-inch Bundt pan.

Combine cake mix, pudding mix, eggs, 1 cup orange juice, oil and orange peel in large mixing bowl. Beat at medium speed with electric mixer for 2 minutes. Pour into prepared pan. Bake 50 to 60 minutes or until toothpick inserted in center comes out clean. Cool 25 minutes in pan. Invert onto serving plate.

Combine sugar and 4 tablespoons orange juice in small saucepan. Simmer 3 minutes. Brush warm glaze on cake.

Makes 12 to 16 servings

TIP

Serve cake with peach ice cream.

Double Chocolate Cream Cake

1 package DUNCAN HINES
Moist Deluxe Butter
Recipe Fudge Cake Mix
1 envelope whipped topping
mix

½ cup chocolate syrup
Maraschino cherries with
stems for garnish

Preheat oven to 375°F. Grease and flour 13×9-inch pan.

Prepare, bake and cool cake as directed on package.

Prepare whipped topping mix as directed on package. Fold in chocolate syrup until blended. Refrigerate until ready to serve.

To serve, spoon topping over cake slices. Garnish with maraschino cherries.   *Makes 12 to 16 servings*

TIP

**For best consistency, chill chocolate
syrup before using.**

Pumpkin Streusel Cake

Streusel

1 cup packed brown sugar
2 teaspoons ground
   cinnamon

⅓ cup butter or margarine,
   softened
1 cup chopped nuts

Cake

1 package DUNCAN HINES
   Moist Deluxe Yellow
   Cake Mix
1 (16-ounce) can solid pack
   pumpkin

3 eggs
¼ cup butter or margarine,
   softened

Preheat oven to 350°F.

Combine sugar and cinnamon in small bowl. Cut in ⅓ cup butter with pastry blender or 2 knives. Stir in nuts; set aside.

Combine cake mix, pumpkin, eggs and ¼ cup butter in large mixing bowl. Beat at medium speed with electric mixer for 2 minutes. Spread half of batter into *ungreased* 13×9-inch pan. Sprinkle half of streusel over batter. Spread remaining batter over streusel. Top with remaining streusel. Bake 40 to 45 minutes or until toothpick inserted in center comes out clean.

Makes 12 to 16 servings

TIP

**Serve warm as a coffeecake or cool as a
dessert topped with whipped topping.**

Double Pineapple Upside-Down Cake

½ cup (1 stick) butter or
    margarine
1 cup packed brown sugar
1 (20-ounce) can pineapple
    slices, drained
  Maraschino cherry halves,
    drained

1 package DUNCAN HINES
    Moist Deluxe Pineapple
    Supreme Cake Mix
Whipped cream

Preheat oven to 350°F.

Place butter in 13×9-inch pan. Place pan in oven to melt butter. Sprinkle with sugar. Arrange pineapple slices and maraschino cherries on sugar mixture.

Prepare cake mix as directed on package. (Do not substitute pineapple juice for water.) Pour batter evenly over fruit. Bake 50 minutes or until toothpick inserted in center comes out clean. Let stand 5 minutes. Invert onto large serving plate or cookie sheet. Serve warm with whipped cream. *Makes 12 to 16 servings*

TIP

This cake is also delicious using DUNCAN HINES Moist Deluxe Yellow Cake Mix.

Dump Cake

1 (20-ounce) can crushed
   pineapple with juice,
   undrained
1 (21-ounce) can cherry pie
   filling
1 package DUNCAN HINES
   Moist Deluxe Yellow
   Cake Mix

1 cup chopped pecans or
   walnuts
½ cup (1 stick) butter or
   margarine, cut into thin
   slices

Preheat oven to 350°F. Grease 13×9-inch pan.

Dump pineapple with juice into pan. Spread evenly. Dump in pie
filling. Spread evenly. Sprinkle cake mix evenly over cherry layer.
Sprinkle pecans over cake mix. Dot with butter. Bake 50 minutes or
until top is lightly browned. Serve warm or at room temperature.

Makes 12 to 16 servings

TIP

**You can use DUNCAN HINES Moist
Deluxe Pineapple Supreme Cake Mix in
place of Moist Deluxe Yellow Cake Mix.**

Dump Cake

Holiday Fruit Cake

1 pound diced candied
   mixed fruits
8 ounces candied cherries,
   cut into halves
4 ounces candied pineapple,
   chopped
1½ cups chopped nuts
1 cup raisins
½ cup all-purpose flour
1 package DUNCAN HINES
   Moist Deluxe Spice Cake
   Mix

1 (4-serving size) package
   vanilla-flavor instant
   pudding and pie filling
   mix
3 eggs
½ cup vegetable oil
¼ cup water
   Light corn syrup, heated,
   for garnish

Preheat oven to 300°F. Grease 10-inch tube pan. Line bottom with aluminum foil.

Reserve ¼ cup assorted candied fruits and nuts for garnish, if desired. Combine remaining candied fruits, nuts and raisins in large bowl. Toss with flour until evenly coated. Set aside.

Combine cake mix, pudding mix, eggs, oil and water in large mixing bowl. Beat at medium speed with electric mixer for 3 minutes (batter will be very stiff). Stir in candied fruit mixture. Spread in prepared pan. Bake 2 hours or until toothpick inserted in center comes out clean. Cool completely in pan. Invert onto serving plate. Peel off foil.

Brush cake with hot corn syrup and decorate with reserved candied fruit pieces and nuts, if desired. To store, wrap in aluminum foil or plastic wrap, or place in airtight container.

Makes 20 to 24 servings

Holiday Fruit Cake

Spice Cake with Rum Caramel Sauce

1 package DUNCAN HINES
   Moist Deluxe Spice Cake
   Mix
¾ cup prepared caramel
   topping

1 tablespoon rum or water
1 teaspoon ground cinnamon
½ cup milk chocolate English
   toffee chips
Whipped cream for garnish

Preheat oven to 350°F. Grease and flour 13×9-inch pan.

Prepare and bake cake as directed on package. Cool cake 10 minutes. Combine topping, rum and cinnamon in small bowl. Spread over warm cake. Top with chips. Serve warm with whipped cream, if desired.   *Makes 12 to 16 servings*

Butterscotch Pudding Cake

1 package DUNCAN HINES
   Moist Deluxe Yellow
   Cake Mix
1 (15¾-ounce) can prepared
   butterscotch pudding

3 eggs
3 tablespoons vegetable oil
1½ cups chopped pecans
1 (12-ounce) package
   butterscotch chips

Preheat oven to 325°F. Grease and flour 13×9-inch pan.

Combine cake mix, pudding, eggs and oil in large mixing bowl. Beat at medium speed with electric mixer for 2 minutes. Pour into prepared pan. Top with pecans and chips. Bake 45 to 50 minutes or until toothpick inserted in center comes out clean. Cool completely in pan.
Makes 12 to 16 servings

Lemony Pound Cake

1 (4-serving size) package lemon-flavor gelatin	4 eggs
¾ cup boiling water	¾ cup vegetable oil
1 package DUNCAN HINES Moist Deluxe Yellow Cake Mix	1 (6-ounce) can frozen lemonade concentrate, thawed
	½ cup granulated sugar

Preheat oven to 350°F. Grease and flour 10-inch tube pan.

Dissolve gelatin in water in large mixing bowl; cool. Stir in cake mix, eggs and oil. Beat at medium speed with electric mixer for 2 minutes. Spoon into prepared pan. Bake 50 minutes or until toothpick inserted in center comes out clean. Mix lemonade concentrate and sugar in small bowl. Pour over hot cake; cool in pan 1 hour. Remove from pan. Cool completely.   *Makes 12 to 16 servings*

TIP

**Serve this cake with fresh or thawed
frozen strawberries for a special dessert.**

Heavenly
COOKIES, BARS & BROWNIES

Spicy Oatmeal Raisin Cookies

1 package DUNCAN HINES Moist Deluxe Spice Cake Mix
4 egg whites
1 cup uncooked quick-cooking oats (not instant or old-fashioned)

½ cup vegetable oil
½ cup raisins

Preheat oven to 350°F. Grease cookie sheets.

Combine cake mix, egg whites, oats and oil in large mixing bowl. Beat at low speed with electric mixer until blended. Stir in raisins. Drop by rounded teaspoonfuls onto prepared cookie sheets.

Bake 7 to 9 minutes or until lightly browned. Cool 1 minute on cookie sheets. Remove to cooling racks; cool completely.

Makes about 4 dozen cookies

Derby Brownies

1 package DUNCAN HINES Walnut Brownie Mix	2 tablespoons bourbon or milk
½ cup (1 stick) butter or margarine, softened	1 container DUNCAN HINES Dark Chocolate Frosting
1 pound confectioners' sugar (about 3½ to 4 cups)	

Preheat oven to 350°F. Grease bottom only of 13×9-inch pan.

Prepare brownie mix as directed on package for cake-like brownies. Pour into prepared pan. Bake 24 to 27 minutes or until set. Cool completely in pan. Beat butter until smooth in large mixing bowl; stir in sugar and bourbon. Beat until smooth and of spreading consistency. Spread over brownies; chill. Top with frosting. Chill 2 to 4 hours. Cut into bars and serve at room temperature.   *Makes 24 brownies*

Chocolate Chip Raspberry Jumbles

1 package DUNCAN HINES Chocolate Chip Cookie Mix	½ cup seedless red raspberry jam

Preheat oven to 350°F.

Prepare chocolate chip cookie mix as directed on package. Reserve ½ cup dough.

Spread remaining dough into *ungreased* 9-inch square pan. Spread jam over base. Drop reserved dough by teaspoonfuls randomly over jam. Bake 20 to 25 minutes or until golden brown. Cool completely in pan. Cut into bars.   *Makes 16 bars*

Derby Brownies

Chocolate Macadamia Cookies

1 package DUNCAN HINES Chocolate Chip Cookie Mix	⅓ cup vegetable oil 1 egg 3 tablespoons water
¼ cup unsweetened cocoa powder	⅔ cup coarsely chopped macadamia nuts

Preheat oven to 375°F.

Combine cookie mix and cocoa in large bowl. Add oil, egg and water. Stir until thoroughly blended. Stir in macadamia nuts. Drop by rounded teaspoonfuls 2 inches apart onto *ungreased* cookie sheets.

Bake 8 to 10 minutes or until set. Cool 1 minute on cookie sheets. Remove to cooling racks. Cool completely.

Makes 3 dozen cookies

Lemon Pecan Crescents

1 package DUNCAN HINES Golden Sugar Cookie Mix	¼ cup all-purpose flour 1 tablespoon grated lemon peel
⅓ cup vegetable oil 2 egg whites ¾ cup toasted pecans, chopped	Confectioners' sugar

Preheat oven to 375°F.

Combine cookie mix, oil, egg whites, pecans, flour and lemon peel in large bowl. Stir until thoroughly blended. Form level half-tablespoonfuls dough into crescent shapes. Place 2 inches apart onto *ungreased* cookie sheets. Bake 8 to 9 minutes or until set but not browned. Cool 2 minutes on cookie sheets. Remove to cooling racks. Roll warm cookies in sugar. Cool completely. Roll cookies again in sugar. Store between layers of waxed paper in airtight container.

Makes about 5 dozen cookies

Chocolate Macadamia Cookies

Glazed Sugar Cookies

Cookies

1 package DUNCAN HINES
Golden Sugar Cookie
Mix

1 egg
¼ cup vegetable oil
1 teaspoon water

Glaze

1½ cups sifted confectioners'
sugar
2 to 3 tablespoons water or
milk
¾ teaspoon vanilla extract

Food coloring (optional)
Red and green sugar
crystals, nonpareils or
cinnamon candies

Preheat oven to 375°F.

Combine cookie mix, egg, oil and 1 teaspoon water in large bowl. Stir until thoroughly blended. Roll dough to ¼-inch thickness on lightly floured surface. Cut dough into desired shapes using floured cookie cutters. Place cookies 2 inches apart onto *ungreased* cookie sheets. Bake 7 to 8 minutes or until edges are light golden brown. Cool 1 minute on cookie sheets. Remove to cooling racks. Cool completely.

Combine sugar, 2 to 3 tablespoons water and vanilla extract in medium bowl. Beat until smooth. Tint glaze with food coloring, if desired. Brush glaze on each cookie with clean pastry brush. Sprinkle cookies with sugar crystals, nonpareils or cinnamon candies before glaze sets. Allow glaze to set before storing between layers of waxed paper in airtight container. *Makes 4 dozen cookies*

TIP

**Use DUNCAN HINES Vanilla Frosting
for a quick glaze. Heat frosting in
opened container in microwave oven at
HIGH for 10 to 15 seconds. Stir well.
Spread on cookies and decorate as
desired before frosting sets.**

Macaroon Brownies

1 package DUNCAN HINES Chewy Fudge Brownie Mix	¼ teaspoon almond extract
2 egg whites	1 cup finely chopped almonds
½ cup granulated sugar	1 cup flaked coconut

Preheat oven to 350°F. Grease bottom only of 13×9-inch pan.

Prepare brownies as directed on package for cake-like brownies. Bake 25 minutes or until set. Place egg whites in medium mixing bowl. Beat at high speed with electric mixer until foamy and double in volume. Beat in sugar gradually, beating until meringue forms firm peaks. Add almond extract. Fold in almonds and coconut. Spread over warm brownies. Bake 12 to 14 minutes or until meringue is set and lightly browned. Cool completely in pan. Cut into bars.

Makes 24 brownies

TIP

Spread the meringue to the edges of the pan to prevent meringue from shrinking.

Lemon Bars

1 package DUNCAN HINES
   Moist Deluxe Lemon
   Supreme Cake Mix
3 eggs, divided
⅓ cup butter-flavor
   shortening
½ cup granulated sugar

¼ cup lemon juice
2 teaspoons grated lemon
   peel
½ teaspoon baking powder
¼ teaspoon salt
   Confectioners' sugar

Preheat oven to 350°F.

Combine cake mix, 1 egg and shortening in large mixing bowl. Beat at low speed with electric mixer until crumbs form. Reserve 1 cup. Pat remaining mixture lightly into *ungreased* 13×9-inch pan. Bake 15 minutes or until lightly browned.

Combine remaining 2 eggs, granulated sugar, lemon juice, lemon peel, baking powder and salt in medium mixing bowl. Beat at medium speed with electric mixer until light and foamy. Pour over hot crust. Sprinkle with reserved crumb mixture.

Bake 15 minutes or until lightly browned. Sprinkle with confectioners' sugar. Cool in pan. Cut into bars.   *Makes 30 to 32 bars*

TIP

**These bars are also delicious using
DUNCAN HINES Moist Deluxe
Yellow Cake Mix.**

Lemon Bars

Golden Gingersnaps

1 package DUNCAN HINES Golden Sugar Cookie Mix	1½ teaspoons ground ginger
	1 teaspoon ground cinnamon
1 egg	½ teaspoon baking soda
1 tablespoon water	¼ cup granulated sugar
1 tablespoon light molasses	1 tablespoon milk
	⅓ cup finely chopped pecans

Preheat oven to 375°F. Grease cookie sheets.

Combine cookie mix, egg, water, molasses, ginger, cinnamon and baking soda in large bowl. Stir until thoroughly blended. Drop by level tablespoonfuls into sugar. Roll to completely cover. Place 2 inches apart onto prepared cookie sheets. Flatten slightly with bottom of drinking glass. Brush tops lightly with milk. Sprinkle with pecans. Bake 9 minutes for chewy cookies or 10 minutes for crisp cookies. Cool 2 minutes on cookie sheets. Remove to cooling racks. Cool completely. Store in airtight container.   *Makes 3 dozen cookies*

Mocha Brownies

1 package DUNCAN HINES Walnut Brownie Mix	2 tablespoons instant coffee granules
1 egg	1 container DUNCAN HINES Chocolate Mocha Frosting
⅓ cup water	
⅓ cup vegetable oil	

Preheat oven to 350°F. Grease bottom only of 13×9-inch pan.

Combine brownie mix, egg, water, oil and coffee granules in large bowl. Mix with spoon until well blended, about 50 strokes. Spread in prepared pan. Bake 25 to 28 minutes or until set. Cool in pan. Spread with frosting; cut into bars.   *Makes 24 brownies*

Golden Gingersnaps

Double Fudge Brownie Bars

1 package DUNCAN HINES
  Double Fudge Brownie
  Mix
2 eggs
⅓ cup water
¼ cup vegetable oil
1 (6-ounce) package
  semisweet chocolate
  chips

1 cup peanut butter chips
½ cup chopped pecans
1 cup flaked coconut
1 (14-ounce) can sweetened
  condensed milk

Preheat oven to 350°F. Grease bottom only of 13×9-inch pan.

Combine brownie mix, contents of fudge packet from mix, eggs, water and oil in large bowl. Stir with spoon until well blended, about 50 strokes. Spread in prepared pan. Bake 18 minutes. Remove from oven. Sprinkle chocolate chips over brownie base, then sprinkle with peanut butter chips, pecans and coconut. Pour milk over top. Bake 22 to 25 minutes or until light golden brown. Cool completely in pan. Cut into bars. *Makes 20 to 24 bars*

TIP

**For a delicious flavor variation,
substitute butterscotch-flavored chips
for the peanut butter chips.**

Double Fudge Brownie Bars

Raspberry Almond Sandwich Cookies

1 package DUNCAN HINES Golden Sugar Cookie Mix	1 tablespoon water
1 egg	³/₄ teaspoon almond extract
¼ cup vegetable oil	1¹/₃ cups sliced natural almonds, broken
	Seedless red raspberry jam

Preheat oven to 375°F.

Combine cookie mix, egg, oil, water and almond extract in large bowl. Stir until thoroughly blended. Drop half of dough by level teaspoonfuls 2 inches apart onto *ungreased* cookie sheets. (Dough will spread during baking to 1¹/₂ to 1³/₄ inches.)

Place almonds on waxed paper. Drop remaining half of dough by level teaspoonfuls onto nuts. Place almond side up 2 inches apart onto *ungreased* cookie sheets.

Bake both plain and almond cookies 6 minutes or until set but not browned. Cool 1 minute on cookie sheets. Remove to cooling racks. Cool completely.

Spread bottoms of plain cookies with jam; top with almond cookies. Press together to make sandwiches. Store in airtight container.

Makes 6 dozen sandwich cookies

Maple Walnut Bars

1 package DUNCAN HINES Moist Deluxe Yellow Cake Mix, divided	1¹/₃ cups MRS. BUTTERWORTH® Maple Syrup
¹/₃ cup butter or margarine, melted	¹/₃ cup packed light brown sugar
4 eggs, divided	¹/₂ teaspoon vanilla extract
	1 cup chopped walnuts

Preheat oven to 350°F. Grease 13×9-inch pan.

Reserve ²/₃ cup cake mix; set aside. Combine remaining cake mix, melted butter and 1 egg in large bowl. Stir until thoroughly blended.

(Mixture will be crumbly.) Press into prepared pan. Bake 15 to 20 minutes or until light golden brown.

Combine reserved cake mix, maple syrup, remaining 3 eggs, sugar and vanilla extract in large mixing bowl. Beat at low speed with electric mixer for 3 minutes. Pour over crust. Sprinkle with walnuts. Bake 30 to 35 minutes or until filling is set. Cool completely in pan. Cut into bars. Store in refrigerator.   *Makes 24 bars*

Fudgy Cookie Squares

Cookie Crust

1 package DUNCAN HINES Chocolate Chip Cookie Mix

⅓ cup vegetable oil
1 egg
3 tablespoons water

Topping

1 (14-ounce) can sweetened condensed milk
1 (12-ounce) package semisweet chocolate chips

2 tablespoons butter or margarine
1 cup chopped walnuts
1 tablespoon vanilla extract
Walnut halves for garnish

Preheat oven to 350°F.

Combine cookie mix, oil, egg and water in large bowl. Stir until thoroughly blended. Spread into *ungreased* 13×9-inch pan. Bake 15 to 20 minutes or until light golden brown. Cool completely in pan.

Combine milk, chips and butter in medium saucepan. Cook on low heat, stirring constantly, until chips are melted. Remove from heat. Add chopped walnuts and vanilla extract; stir until blended. Spread over cookie crust. Score into squares with tip of knife. Place walnut half on top of each square, if desired. Refrigerate until firm. Cut into squares. Refrigerate until ready to serve.   *Makes 24 to 48 squares*

German Chocolate Brownies

1 package DUNCAN HINES
   Milk Chocolate Chunk
   Brownie Mix
2 eggs
⅓ cup water
⅓ cup vegetable oil
½ cup packed brown sugar

2 tablespoons butter or
   margarine, softened
1 tablespoon all-purpose
   flour
½ cup chopped pecans
½ cup flaked coconut

Preheat oven to 350°F. Grease bottom only of 13×9-inch pan.

Combine brownie mix, eggs, water and oil in large bowl. Stir with spoon until well blended, about 50 strokes. Spread into prepared pan.

Combine sugar, butter and flour in small bowl. Mix until well blended. Stir in pecans and coconut. Sprinkle mixture over batter. Bake 25 to 30 minutes or until topping is browned. Cool completely in pan. Cut into bars.   *Makes 24 brownies*

TIP

Always mix brownies by hand. Never use an electric mixer.

German Chocolate Brownies

Peanut Butter Knockouts

1 package DUNCAN HINES Peanut Butter Cookie Mix	Dash salt (optional)
1 whole egg	½ cup semisweet mini chocolate chips (optional)
1 (3-ounce) package cream cheese, softened	½ cup semisweet chocolate chips
¼ cup creamy peanut butter	2 teaspoons shortening
1 egg yolk	
2½ tablespoons granulated sugar	

Preheat oven to 375°F.

Combine cookie mix, contents of peanut butter packet from mix and whole egg in large bowl. Stir until thoroughly blended. Shape dough into 36 (about 1-inch) balls. Place 2 inches apart onto *ungreased* cookie sheets. Press thumb gently in center of each cookie.

Combine cream cheese, peanut butter, egg yolk, sugar and salt in medium bowl. Beat at medium speed with electric mixer until blended. Stir in mini chocolate chips, if desired. Fill center of each cookie with rounded teaspoonful of filling. Bake 8 to 10 minutes or until light golden brown. Cool 2 minutes on cookie sheets. Remove to cooling racks. Cool completely.

Place chocolate chips and shortening in small resealable plastic bag; seal. Place bag in bowl of hot water for several minutes. Dry bag with towel. Knead bag until contents are blended and chocolate is smooth. Snip tiny hole in corner of bag. Drizzle contents over cookies. Allow drizzle to set before storing cookies between layers of waxed paper in airtight container. *Makes 3 dozen cookies*

Peanut Butter Knockouts

Cherry Surprises

1 package DUNCAN HINES Golden Sugar Cookie Mix	½ cup semisweet chocolate chips
36 to 42 candied cherries	1 teaspoon shortening

Preheat oven to 375°F. Grease cookie sheets.

Prepare cookie mix as directed on package. Shape thin layer of dough around each cherry. Place 2 inches apart onto prepared cookie sheets. Bake 8 minutes or until set but not browned. Cool 1 minute on cookie sheets. Remove to cooling racks. Cool completely.

Combine chips and shortening in small resealable plastic bag. Place bag in bowl of hot water for several minutes. Dry bag with towel. Knead until blended and chocolate is smooth. Snip pinpoint hole in corner of bag. Drizzle chocolate over cookies. Allow drizzle to set before storing between layers of waxed paper in airtight container.

Makes 3 to 3½ dozen cookies

Tip: Well-drained maraschino cherries may be substituted for candied cherries.

Gingerbread Men

1 package DUNCAN HINES Moist Deluxe Spice Cake Mix	⅓ cup vegetable oil
½ cup all-purpose flour	⅓ cup dark molasses
2 eggs	2 teaspoons ground ginger
	Raisins for decorations

Combine cake mix, flour, eggs, oil, molasses and ginger in large bowl (mixture will be soft). Refrigerate 2 hours.

Preheat oven to 375°F.

Roll dough to ¼-inch thickness on lightly floured surface. Cut with gingerbread man cookie cutter. Place 3 inches apart onto *ungreased* cookie sheet. Decorate with raisins.

Bake 8 to 10 minutes or until edges start to brown. Remove immediately to cooling rack.

Makes 12 to 14 six-inch gingerbread men

Tip: To make holes for hanging cookie ornaments, push straw or meat skewer in head section of cookies before baking.

Chocolate Peanut Butter Cookies

1 package DUNCAN HINES Moist Deluxe Devil's Food Cake Mix	2 eggs
	2 tablespoons milk
	1 cup candy-coated peanut butter pieces
¾ cup crunchy peanut butter	

Preheat oven to 350°F. Grease cookie sheets.

Combine cake mix, peanut butter, eggs and milk in large mixing bowl. Beat at low speed with electric mixer until blended. Stir in peanut butter pieces.

Drop dough by slightly rounded tablespoonfuls onto prepared cookie sheets. Bake 7 to 9 minutes or until lightly browned. Cool 2 minutes on cookie sheets. Remove to cooling racks.

Makes about 3½ dozen cookies

Tip: You can use 1 cup peanut butter chips in place of peanut butter pieces.

Scrumptious DESSERTS

Creamy Banana Toffee Dessert

1 package DUNCAN HINES Moist Deluxe Butter Recipe Golden Cake Mix	1½ cups milk
1 (4-serving size) package banana cream-flavor instant pudding and pie filling mix	1 (8-ounce) container frozen non-dairy whipped topping, thawed
	3 medium bananas, sliced
	¾ cup English toffee bits

Preheat oven to 375°F. Grease and flour 10-inch tube pan.

Prepare, bake and cool cake as directed on package. Meanwhile, combine pudding mix and milk in medium bowl. Chill 5 minutes. Fold in whipped topping. Chill while cake cools.

To assemble, cut cake into 12 slices. Place 6 cake slices in 3-quart clear glass bowl. Top with half of bananas, pudding and toffee bits. Repeat layering. Chill until ready to serve.

Makes 12 to 14 servings

Angel Almond Cupcakes

1 package DUNCAN HINES Angel Food Cake Mix 1¼ cups water 2 teaspoons almond extract	1 container DUNCAN HINES Wild Cherry Vanilla Frosting

Preheat oven to 350°F.

Combine cake mix, water and almond extract in large mixing bowl. Beat at low speed with electric mixer until moistened. Beat at medium speed for 1 minute. Line medium muffin pans with paper baking cups. Fill muffin cups two-thirds full. Bake 20 to 25 minutes or until golden brown, cracked and dry. Remove from muffin pans. Cool completely. Frost with frosting.　　　　　　　　*Makes 30 to 32 cupcakes*

Strawberry Brownie Shortcake

1 package DUNCAN HINES Double Fudge Brownie Mix 1 (4-serving size) package vanilla-flavor instant pudding and pie filling mix	1½ cups milk 2 cups frozen non-dairy whipped topping, thawed 1 quart fresh strawberries, hulled and halved

Preheat oven to 350°F. Grease bottoms and sides of two 9-inch round cake pans.

Prepare brownie mix as directed on package for cake-like brownies; pour into prepared pans. Bake 20 to 25 minutes or until top springs back when touched. Cool 10 minutes. Remove from pans; cool completely. Meanwhile, stir pudding mix and milk in medium bowl; mix well. Chill 5 minutes. Fold in whipped topping. Chill. To serve, place one brownie layer on plate. Top with half each of pudding mixture and strawberries. Repeat. Garnish as desired.

Makes 8 to 10 servings

Angel Almond Cupcakes

Grasshopper Dessert

Crust

1 package DUNCAN HINES
Moist Deluxe Dark
Chocolate Fudge Cake
Mix, divided

1 egg
½ cup (1 stick) butter or
margarine, softened

Filling

3 cups miniature
marshmallows
½ cup milk
⅓ cup green crème de
menthe

2 tablespoons white crème
de cacao
1½ cups whipping cream,
chilled

Preheat oven to 350°F. Grease and flour 13×9-inch pan. Remove
½ cup cake mix and spread into 8-inch *ungreased* baking pan. Toast
in oven 7 minutes. Cool.

Combine remaining cake mix, egg and butter in large bowl. Mix until
crumbs form. Press lightly into prepared pan. Bake 15 minutes. Cool.

Heat marshmallows and milk in medium saucepan over low heat. Stir
constantly until marshmallows melt. Refrigerate until thickened. Stir
crème de menthe and crème de cacao into marshmallow mixture.

Beat whipping cream until stiff in large bowl. Fold in marshmallow
mixture. Pour into crust. Dust top with cooled toasted cake mix.
Refrigerate until ready to serve. Cut into squares.

Makes 12 servings

TIP

**To quickly chill marshmallow mixture,
pour mixture into medium bowl; place
in larger bowl of ice water and
refrigerate. Stir occasionally.**

Angel Strawberry Bavarian

1 package DUNCAN HINES
   Angel Food Cake Mix
1 (10-ounce) package frozen
   sweetened sliced
   strawberries, thawed
1 (4-serving size) package
   strawberry-flavored
   gelatin
1 cup boiling water

2½ cups whipping cream,
   chilled, divided
2½ tablespoons confectioners'
   sugar
¾ teaspoon vanilla extract
4 fresh strawberries, sliced
   and fanned, for garnish
Mint leaves for garnish

Preheat oven to 375°F.

Prepare, bake and cool cake as directed on package. Cut cake into 1-inch cubes. Drain thawed strawberries, reserving juice.

Combine gelatin and boiling water in small bowl. Stir until gelatin is dissolved. Add enough water to strawberry juice to measure 1 cup; stir into gelatin. Refrigerate until gelatin is slightly thickened. Beat gelatin until foamy.

Beat 1 cup whipping cream until stiff peaks form in large bowl. Fold into gelatin along with strawberries.

Alternate layers of cake cubes and strawberry mixture into 10-inch tube pan. Press lightly. Cover. Refrigerate overnight.

Unmold cake onto serving plate. Beat remaining 1½ cups whipping cream, sugar and vanilla extract until stiff peaks form. Frost sides and top of cake. Refrigerate until ready to serve. Garnish with fresh strawberries and mint leaves. *Makes 12 to 16 servings*

Brownie Ice Cream Pie

1 package DUNCAN HINES
   Chewy Fudge Brownie
   Mix
2 eggs
½ cup vegetable oil
¼ cup water
¾ cup semisweet chocolate
   chips

1 (9-inch) unbaked pastry
   crust
1 (10-ounce) package frozen
   sweetened sliced
   strawberries
Vanilla ice cream

Preheat oven to 350°F.

Combine brownie mix, eggs, oil and water in large bowl. Stir with spoon until well blended, about 50 strokes. Stir in chips. Spoon into crust. Bake 40 to 45 minutes or until set. Cool completely. Purée strawberries in food processor or blender. Cut pie into wedges. Serve with ice cream and puréed strawberries.   *Makes 8 servings*

Brownie Candy Cups

1 package DUNCAN HINES
   Double Fudge Brownie
   Mix
2 eggs
⅓ cup water

¼ cup vegetable oil
30 miniature peanut butter
   cup candies

Preheat oven to 350°F. Place 30 (2-inch) foil liners in muffin pans or on cookie sheets.

Combine brownie mix, fudge packet from mix, eggs, water and oil in large bowl. Stir with spoon until well blended, about 50 strokes. Place 2 level tablespoonfuls batter into each foil liner. Bake 10 minutes. Remove from oven. Push 1 peanut butter cup candy in center of each cupcake until even with surface of cupcake. Bake 5 to 7 minutes or until candy is softened. Remove to cooling racks. Cool completely.

Makes 30 brownie cups

Brownie Ice Cream Pie

Chocolate Chip Cheesecake

1 package DUNCAN HINES
   Moist Deluxe Devil's
   Food Cake Mix
½ cup vegetable oil
3 (8-ounce) packages cream
   cheese, softened
1½ cups granulated sugar
1 cup sour cream

1½ teaspoons vanilla extract
4 eggs, lightly beaten
¾ cup semisweet mini
   chocolate chips, divided
1 teaspoon all-purpose flour

Preheat oven to 350°F. Grease 10-inch springform pan.

Combine cake mix and oil in large bowl. Mix well. Press onto bottom of prepared pan. Bake 22 to 25 minutes or until set. Remove from oven. *Increase oven temperature to 450°F.*

Place cream cheese in large mixing bowl. Beat at low speed with electric mixer, adding sugar gradually. Add sour cream and vanilla extract, mixing until blended. Add eggs, mixing only until incorporated. Toss ½ cup chocolate chips with flour. Fold into cream cheese mixture. Pour filling onto crust. Sprinkle with remaining ¼ cup chocolate chips. Bake 5 to 7 minutes. *Reduce oven temperature to 250°F.* Bake 60 to 65 minutes or until set. Loosen cake from side of pan with knife or spatula. Cool completely in pan on cooling rack. Refrigerate until ready to serve. Remove side of pan.

Makes 12 to 16 servings

TIP

Place pan of water on bottom shelf of oven during baking to prevent cheesecake from cracking.

Chocolate Chip Cheesecake

Lemon Cheesecake with Raspberry Sauce

Crust

1 package DUNCAN HINES
    Moist Deluxe Lemon
    Supreme Cake Mix

½ cup vegetable oil
⅓ cup finely chopped pecans

Filling

3 (8-ounce) packages cream
    cheese, softened
¾ cup granulated sugar
2 tablespoons lemon juice

1 teaspoon grated lemon
    peel
3 eggs, lightly beaten

Raspberry Sauce

1 (12-ounce) package frozen
    dry pack red raspberries,
    thawed
⅓ cup granulated sugar

Fresh raspberries, lemon
    slices and mint leaves
    for garnish

Preheat oven to 350°F. Grease 10-inch springform pan. Combine cake mix and oil in large bowl. Mix well. Stir in pecans. Press mixture onto bottom of prepared pan. Bake about 20 minutes or until light golden brown. Remove from oven. *Increase oven temperature to 450°F.*

Place cream cheese in large mixing bowl. Beat at low speed with electric mixer, adding ¾ cup sugar gradually. Add lemon juice and lemon peel. Add eggs, mixing only until incorporated. Pour filling into crust. Bake 5 to 7 minutes. *Reduce oven temperature to 250°F.* Bake 30 minutes or until set. Loosen cake from side of pan with knife or spatula. Cool completely in pan on cooling rack. Refrigerate 2 hours or until ready to serve. Remove side of pan.

Combine thawed raspberries and ⅓ cup sugar in small saucepan. Bring to a boil. Simmer until berries are soft. Strain through sieve into small bowl to remove seeds. Cool completely. To serve, garnish cheesecake with fresh raspberries, lemon slices and mint leaves. Cut into slices and serve with raspberry sauce.

Makes 12 to 16 servings

Creamy Eggnog Dessert

Crust

1 package DUNCAN HINES
Moist Deluxe Swiss
Chocolate Cake Mix

½ cup (1 stick) butter or
margarine, melted
½ cup chopped pecans

Filling

1 (8-ounce) package cream
cheese, softened

1 cup granulated sugar

Topping

1 (12-ounce) container
frozen non-dairy
whipped topping,
thawed, divided
2 (4-serving size) packages
French vanilla-flavor
instant pudding and pie
filling mix

3 cups cold milk
¼ teaspoon rum extract
¼ teaspoon ground nutmeg

Preheat oven to 350°F.

Combine cake mix, melted butter and pecans. Reserve ½ cup mixture.
Press remaining mixture onto bottom of 13×9-inch pan. Bake 15 to
20 minutes or until surface is firm. Cool. Toast reserved ½ cup mixture
on cookie sheet 3 to 4 minutes, stirring once. Cool completely. Break
lumps with fork to make small crumbs.

Combine cream cheese and sugar in large bowl; beat until smooth.
Stir in 1 cup whipped topping. Spread over cooled crust. Refrigerate.
Combine pudding mix and milk; beat 1 minute. Add rum extract and
nutmeg. Spread over cheese layer. Spread remaining whipped topping
over pudding layer. Sprinkle with reserved crumbs. Refrigerate at least
2 hours.   *Makes 12 to 16 servings*

Sugar Cookie Pizza

1 package DUNCAN HINES Golden Sugar Cookie Mix	**1 container DUNCAN HINES Vanilla or Chocolate Frosting (optional)**
½ cup semisweet mini chocolate coated candy pieces	

Preheat oven to 350°F.

Prepare cookie mix as directed on package. Spread onto lightly greased 12-inch pizza pan. Sprinkle candy pieces evenly over cookie dough; press down gently. Bake 15 to 20 minutes or until golden brown. Cool 3 to 4 minutes in pan. Remove from pan; cool completely. Decorate with frosting, if desired. *Makes 12 servings*

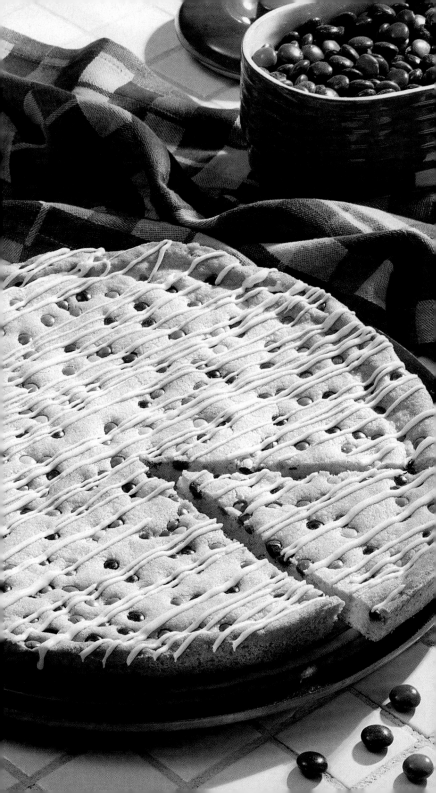

Chocolate Chip Waffles

1 package DUNCAN HINES Chocolate Chip Muffin Mix	2 eggs
¾ cup all-purpose flour	5 tablespoons butter or margarine, melted
1 teaspoon baking powder	Confectioners' sugar (optional)
1¾ cups milk	

Preheat and lightly grease waffle iron according to manufacturer's directions.

Combine muffin mix, flour and baking powder in large bowl. Add milk, eggs and melted butter. Stir until moistened, about 50 strokes. Pour batter onto center grids of preheated waffle iron. Bake according to manufacturer's directions until golden brown. Remove baked waffle carefully with fork. Repeat with remaining batter. Dust lightly with sugar, if desired. Top with fresh fruit, syrup, grated chocolate or whipped cream, if desired. *Makes 10 to 12 waffles*

Golden Oatmeal Muffins

1 package DUNCAN HINES Moist Deluxe Butter Recipe Golden Cake Mix	¼ teaspoon salt
	¾ cup milk
1 cup uncooked quick-cooking oats (not instant or old-fashioned)	2 eggs, lightly beaten
	2 tablespoons butter or margarine, melted

Preheat oven to 400°F. Grease 24 (2½-inch) muffin cups (or use paper liners).

Combine cake mix, oats and salt in large bowl. Add milk, eggs and melted butter; stir until moistened. Fill muffin cups two-thirds full. Bake 13 minutes or until golden brown. Cool in pan 5 to 10 minutes. Loosen carefully before removing from pan. Serve with honey or your favorite jam. *Makes 2 dozen muffins*

Chocolate Chip Waffles

Lemon Cranberry Loaves

1¼ cups finely chopped fresh
    cranberries
½ cup finely chopped
    walnuts
¼ cup granulated sugar
1 package DUNCAN HINES
    Moist Deluxe Lemon
    Supreme Cake Mix

¾ cup milk
1 (3-ounce) package cream
    cheese, softened
4 eggs
    Confectioners' sugar

Preheat oven to 350°F. Grease and flour two 8½×4½-inch loaf pans.

Stir together cranberries, walnuts and granulated sugar in large bowl; set aside.

Combine cake mix, milk and cream cheese in large mixing bowl. Beat at medium speed with electric mixer for 2 minutes. Add eggs, 1 at a time, beating for 2 minutes. Fold in cranberry mixture. Pour into prepared pans. Bake 45 to 50 minutes or until toothpick inserted in centers comes out clean. Cool in pans 15 minutes. Loosen loaves from pans. Invert onto cooling rack. Turn right side up. Cool completely. Dust with confectioners' sugar. *Makes 24 slices*

Tip: To quickly chop cranberries or walnuts, use food processor fitted with steel blade and pulse until evenly chopped.

Peachy Blueberry Crunch

1 package DUNCAN HINES
    Bakery Style Blueberry
    Muffin Mix
4 cups sliced peeled peaches
    (about 4 large)
½ cup water
3 tablespoons packed brown
    sugar

½ cup chopped pecans
⅓ cup butter or margarine,
    melted
    Whipped topping or ice
    cream (optional)

Preheat oven to 350°F.

Rinse blueberries from mix with cold water and drain.

Arrange peach slices into *ungreased* 9-inch square pan. Sprinkle blueberries over peaches. Combine water and sugar in small bowl. Pour over fruit.

Combine muffin mix, pecans and melted butter in large bowl. Stir until thoroughly blended (mixture will be crumbly). Sprinkle crumb mixture over fruit. Sprinkle contents of topping packet from mix over crumb mixture. Bake 50 to 55 minutes or until lightly browned and bubbly. Serve warm with whipped topping, if desired.

Makes 9 servings

Truffles

1 container DUNCAN HINES Milk Chocolate Frosting	1 cup pecan halves, divided
	1 cup semisweet chocolate chips
2½ cups confectioners' sugar	3 tablespoons shortening

Combine frosting and sugar in large mixing bowl. Stir with wooden spoon until thoroughly blended. Cover ⅔ cup pecan halves with 1 tablespoon frosting mixture each. Roll into 1-inch balls; set aside. Chop remaining pecans; set aside. Place chocolate chips and shortening in 2-cup glass measuring cup. Microwave at MEDIUM (50% power) for 2 minutes; stir. Microwave 1 minute at MEDIUM; stir until smooth. Dip one candy ball into chocolate mixture until completely covered. Remove with fork to cooling rack. Sprinkle top with chopped pecans. Repeat until all candy balls are covered. Allow to stand until chocolate mixture is set.

Makes about 3 dozen candies

Cranberry Cobbler

2 (16-ounce) cans sliced
   peaches in light syrup,
   drained
1 (16-ounce) can whole
   berry cranberry sauce
1 package DUNCAN HINES
   Cinnamon Swirl Muffin
   Mix

½ cup chopped pecans
⅓ cup butter or margarine,
   melted
   Whipped topping or ice
   cream

Preheat oven to 350°F.

Cut peach slices in half lengthwise. Combine peach slices and cranberry sauce in *ungreased* 9-inch square pan. Knead swirl packet from mix for 10 seconds. Squeeze contents evenly over fruit.

Combine muffin mix, contents of topping packet from mix and pecans in large bowl. Add melted butter. Stir until thoroughly blended (mixture will be crumbly). Sprinkle crumbs over fruit. Bake 40 to 45 minutes or until lightly browned and bubbly. Serve warm with whipped topping. *Makes 9 servings*

TIP

Store leftovers in the refrigerator. Reheat in microwave oven to serve warm.

Cranberry Cobbler

Nutty Blueberry Muffins

1 package DUNCAN HINES
   Blueberry Muffin Mix
2 egg whites

½ cup water
⅓ cup chopped pecans

Preheat oven to 400°F. Grease 2½-inch muffin cups (or use paper liners).

Rinse blueberries from mix with cold water and drain.

Pour muffin mix into large bowl. Break up any lumps. Add egg whites and water. Stir until moistened, about 50 strokes. Stir in pecans; fold in blueberries.

For large muffins, fill cups two-thirds full. Bake 17 to 22 minutes or until toothpick inserted in center comes out clean. (For medium muffins, fill cups half full. Bake 15 to 20 minutes.) Cool in pan 5 to 10 minutes. Loosen carefully before removing from pan.

Makes 8 large or 12 medium muffins

TIP

To reheat leftover muffins, wrap the muffins tightly in foil. Place them in a 400°F oven for 10 to 15 minutes.

Nutty Blueberry Muffins

Blueberry Poppy Seed Coffeecake with Lemon Sauce

Coffeecake

1 package DUNCAN HINES
  Bakery Style Blueberry
  Muffin Mix
½ teaspoon baking powder

1 egg
⅔ cup water
2 tablespoons poppy seeds
½ teaspoon ground cinnamon

Lemon Sauce

1 cup granulated sugar
½ cup (1 stick) butter or
  margarine, cut into
  pieces
¼ cup water

3 tablespoons lemon juice
1 egg, lightly beaten
1 teaspoon grated lemon
  peel
Lemon slices for garnish

Preheat oven to 400°F. Grease 8- or 9-inch square pan.

Rinse blueberries from mix with cold water and drain.

Combine muffin mix and baking powder in medium bowl. Break up any lumps; stir to blend. Add 1 egg and ⅔ cup water. Fold in blueberries and poppy seeds. Spread into prepared pan.

Combine cinnamon and contents of topping packet from mix in small bowl. Sprinkle over batter. Bake 25 to 28 minutes or until toothpick inserted in center comes out clean.

Combine sugar, butter, ¼ cup water, lemon juice, 1 beaten egg and lemon peel in saucepan. Cook on medium heat, stirring constantly, until thickened. Serve warm with slices of coffeecake. Garnish with lemon slices, if desired.   *Makes 9 servings*

RECIPE INDEX

93

RECIPE INDEX

PRODUCT INDEX

PRODUCT INDEX